curiousabout

HORSES

BY JILL SHERMAN

AMICUS · AMICUS INK

What are you

curious about?

CHAPTER THREE

Horse Behavior
PAGE
16

Curious About is published
by Amicus and Amicus Ink
P.O. Box 227
Mankato, MN 56002
www.amicuspublishing.us

Editor: Alissa Thielges
Series Designer: Kathleen Petelinsek
Book Designer: Ciara Beitlich
Photo researcher: Bridget Prehn

Library of Congress Cataloging-in-Publication Data
Names: Sherman, Jill, author.
Title: Curious about horses / by Jill Sherman.
Description: Mankato, MN : Amicus, [2021] | Series: Curious
about pets | Includes bibliographical references and index. |
Audience: Ages 6–9 | Audience: Grades 2–3
Identifiers: LCCN 2019053826 (print) | LCCN 2019053827
(ebook) | ISBN 9781681519685 (library binding) | ISBN
9781681526157 (paperback) | ISBN 9781645490531 (pdf)
Subjects: LCSH: Horses—Juvenile literature.
Classification: LCC SF302.S535 2021 (print) | LCC SF302
(ebook) | DDC 636.1—dc23
LC record available at https://lccn.loc.gov/2019053826
LC ebook record available at https://lccn.loc.gov/2019053827

Photos © iStock/Kerrick cover, 1; iStock/Perkus 2 (left), 5; iStock/
Don White 2 (right), 14; Shutterstock/pukpui228 3, 20; iStock/
ronniechua 6–7; iStock/winhorse 9 (top); Shutterstock/M.Style 9
(horse icon); Shutterstock/Aleks Melnik 9 (hay icon); Shutterstock/
acceptphoto 10, 11; iStock/magbug 12; Shutterstock/
Marie Charouzova 13; iStock/olenalyzun 15; Shutterstock/
Zuzule 16–17; Shutterstock/Viktoriia Bondarenko 18–19;
Shutterstock/Lenkadan 21 (American quarter); Dreamstime/
Viacheslav Nemyrivskyi 21 (Arabian); 123RF/Dimitar Marinov
21 (Thoroughbred); iStock/jeanma85 21 (Appaloosa); Alamy/
WILDLIFE GmbH 21 (Morgan)

CHAPTER ONE

What do you do with a pet horse?

Some horses have jobs. They help farmers or are used as transportation. Many people ride horses for fun or in competitions. People care deeply for their horses. They are beloved friends.

Jumping competitions are all about speed and agility.

Are there wild horses?

Wild horses cross a river
in Alberta, Canada.

Yes. They are **feral** horses. They were once owned but escaped. Now they roam free. People capture and **tame** these horses. Taming takes time and patience. You have to earn the horse's trust.

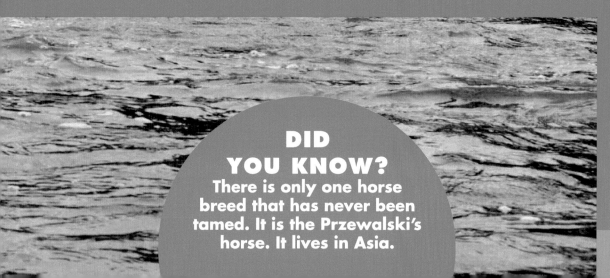

DID YOU KNOW?
There is only one horse breed that has never been tamed. It is the Przewalski's horse. It lives in Asia.

Where do you keep a horse?

A horse needs a lot of space. It is a big animal and needs room to run around. An outside **pasture** is a good home. It can graze and be with other horses. Most people keep their horse in a **stable**. It is a warm and safe place at night. During the day, the horse is let outside.

A stable can hold many horses.

DID YOU KNOW?
It costs a lot to keep a horse for a year.

Food
$1,155

Vet
$480

Farrier
$650

Boarding
$4,800

Average costs based on numbers from *The Horse*, a national magazine about horses.

How do you tell a horse where to go?

A well-trained horse
responds to a soft touch.

On a horse, the rider uses the **reins**. They pull the reins gently to say which way to go. They also press their leg into the horse's side. Horses are very **sensitive**. A small touch is all that's needed. Pulling too hard could upset a horse.

CHAPTER TWO

Why do horses swish their tails?

This horse's tail is telling you to back off.

Swish, swish, flick. Horses move their tails all the time. It keeps away pesky bugs. It is also important for communication. If the tail starts swishing quickly, stand back. That horse could be annoyed or angry. It may kick or **buck**.

A horse can communicate its mood with its tail—and shoo flies away!

This horse is relaxed.

How can I tell what a horse is feeling?

Watch out—this horse is scared.

You watch its body language. A happy horse is calm. Its jaw, nostrils, and lips are relaxed. One of its back legs may be bent. This is a resting state. Is the horse standing stiff or leaning away? Are its ears flicking around? It may be feeling scared or irritated.

CHAPTER THREE

Why do horses kick out with their legs?

Do not approach a kicking horse.

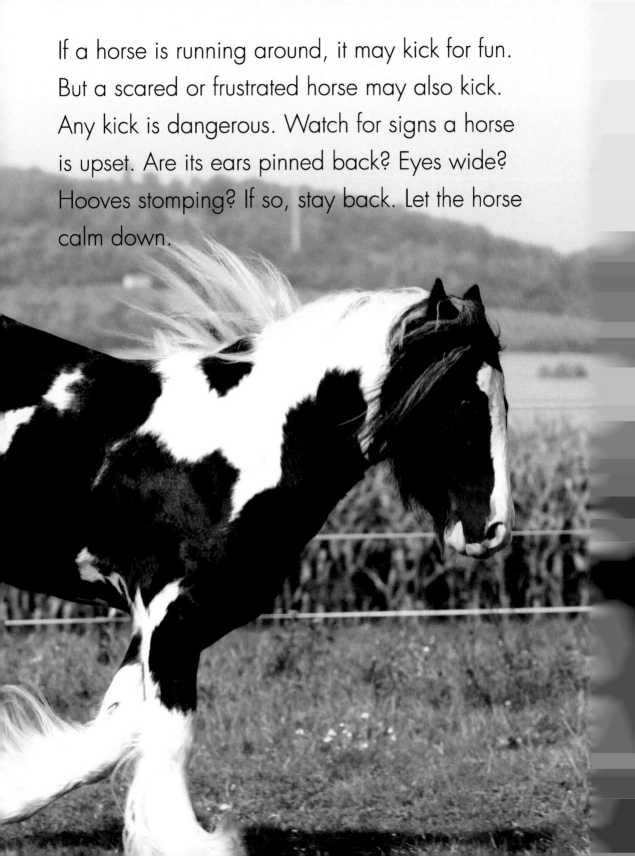

If a horse is running around, it may kick for fun. But a scared or frustrated horse may also kick. Any kick is dangerous. Watch for signs a horse is upset. Are its ears pinned back? Eyes wide? Hooves stomping? If so, stay back. Let the horse calm down.

What kind of exercise does a horse need?

Like kids at recess, horses get exercise when playing.

Horses are very active. They need room to move around every day. A horse should be let out with other horses. They will walk around for hours. If the pasture is big, this is good exercise. If not, walking or riding your horse will give it exercise.

DID YOU KNOW?
The two fastest breeds are the Quarter Horse and the Thoroughbred. They are used in horse races.

Horses doze throughout the day.

Do horses sleep standing up?

Sometimes. They nap in this position. Don't worry, they don't fall down. Their legs lock up. This keeps them from falling over. Resting this way helps them avoid danger. If a noise spooks them, they can run away quickly. When a horse needs a deep sleep, it lies down.

AMERICAN QUARTER HORSE

ARABIAN

THOROUGHBRED

APPALOOSA

MORGAN

STAY CURIOUS!

ASK MORE QUESTIONS

I want a horse. What breed would be best for me?

Where are wild horses in America?

Try a BIG QUESTION: Do horses like to be ridden?

SEARCH FOR ANSWERS

Search the library catalog or the Internet.
A librarian, teacher, or parent can help you.

Using Keywords
Find the looking glass.

Keywords are the most important words in your question.

?

If you want to know about:
- different types of horses, type: HORSE BREEDS
- wild horses, type: WILD HORSES

FIND GOOD SOURCES

Here are some good, safe sources you can use in your research.
Your librarian can help you find more.

Books
Horses
by Quinn M. Arnold, 2020.

Horses from Head to Tail
by Emmett Martin, 2021.

Internet Sites
4-H | Horse
https://4-h.org/parents/curriculum/horse/
4-H is a national organization for kids that offers free resources about horses.

National Geographic Kids | Przewalski's horse
https://kids.nationalgeographic.com/animals/mammals/przewalskis-horse/
National Geographic is a respected source of journalism for science and history. Be aware it may have ads.

Every effort has been made to ensure that these websites are appropriate for children. However, because of the nature of the Internet, it is impossible to guarantee that these sites will remain active indefinitely or that their contents will not be altered.

SHARE AND TAKE ACTION

Take horseback riding lessons.
Learn how to work safely with horses.

Visit horse stables.
Learn about proper horse care.

Go to a horse show or a riding event.
Ask the riders how they trained for the event.

GLOSSARY

buck When a horse springs into the air with its back arched or back legs kicking.

farrier A person who specializes in hoof care for horses' feet. They usually trim and put horse shoes on the hooves.

feral An animal that has escaped from its owners and lives freely, or its wild offspring.

pasture A grassy area of land used for grazing animals.

reins Straps used to control an animal.

sensitive Able to quickly detect and respond to slight changes or signals.

stable A building where horses are fed and sheltered.

tame Gentle and not afraid around people; not wild.

INDEX

About the Author

Jill Sherman is a children's book author living in Brooklyn, New York. She has a pet dog named Reed, whom she spoils endlessly. Reed prefers cuddling on the couch to playing at the dog park, and Jill is perfectly happy with that.